Perspectives

Food
What's Good? What's Bad?

Series Consultant: Linda Hoyt

Flying Start
to Literacy®

Contents

Introduction

What's good?   What's bad?
Do you know what you're eating?

Eat more of this!   Eat less of that!   Everyone eats too much sugar or too much fat!   Sometimes, it's hard to know what the "good" and "bad" foods really are.

With so much information, how do you decide?

10 superfoods

Written by Robin Cruise

People often say: "You are what you eat." That doesn't mean that if you eat a banana, you'll turn into one.

But it does mean the foods you choose to eat can affect how you feel and look — and even how you think.

These 10 superfoods are good choices — and delicious, too. What do you notice about these foods?

Oranges

These juicy fruits are vitamin C superstars! This vitamin can help keep your heart healthy and fight off germs. Oranges are a good source of fibre, which helps you digest the food you eat.

Eggs

Eggs have a lot of protein, which is like fuel that keeps the body moving. It also helps build muscles and strong bones, and keeps your skin and blood healthy.

Oats

These grains are loaded with vitamins and minerals. They also have a lot of fibre and keep your heart healthy.

Yogurt

Yogurt is a milk-based food that helps build strong bones. It can help with digesting food.

Berries

Berries are good sources of fibre. They contain vitamins and minerals that keep you healthy. And they fill you up when you're hungry.

Avocados

This amazing fruit bursts with more than a dozen vitamins. Avocados are good for your skin, eyes and brain. They also boost strength and help your muscles, including your heart, work well.

Nuts

Nuts make good snacks. They are good sources of protein and fibre. Protein can give you energy. Fibre stops you feeling hungry and helps you digest the food you eat.

Spinach

Spinach has lots of vitamin A for healthy eyes, skin and bones, and vitamin C for your heart and for fighting germs.

Broccoli

This green vegetable keeps your body healthy. It is loaded with vitamins and minerals. Broccoli may even help keep your brain sharp.

Sweet potatoes

This vegetable can fill you up without puffing you out! It's high in fibre, but it contains no fat.

Speak out!

Read what these students have to say about eating healthily.

I always have to check the labels on food because I'm allergic to gluten and dairy foods. If I eat food with gluten in it, I get really bad stomach aches. And if I eat dairy foods, I swell up. I've been allergic for six years now, since I was four. Imagine life without cupcakes!

We need to eat foods that are not processed. The reason? Because if you eat processed food, you don't know what you're eating. You might be eating something that has chemicals, or you might be eating fruit with mild poison that will harm you.

I think we have the right to eat well. Lots of fruit and vegetables have been sprayed with chemicals. Many of these chemicals are bad for us. There is the same problem with chickens. They are pumped with artificial flavours and chemicals, which, when you think about it, is gross.

I am a vegetarian, so eating meat is bad for me.

We all need protein, and for many people, they get it by eating meat. I get protein from eggs, beans and tofu.

Natural sugar vs. added sugar

Written by Elizabeth Preston

Most foods naturally contain sugar, and sugar gives us energy. But food makers often add more sugar to make their foods sweeter. It is recommended that kids should have no more than six teaspoons of *added* sugar a day.

How much added sugar do you eat every day? Are you surprised? How could you eat less sugar?

Some of our favourite foods have a lot of sugar!

carrot

1 teaspoon of sugar

apple

5 teaspoons of sugar

fruit smoothie

20 teaspoons of sugar

soft drink

9 teaspoons of sugar

glass of orange juice

5 teaspoons of sugar

sports drink

9 teaspoons of sugar

packet of tomato sauce

1 teaspoon of sugar

muffin

8 teaspoons of sugar

Natural sugar

glass of milk
3 teaspoons of sugar

small tub of natural yogurt
3 teaspoons of sugar

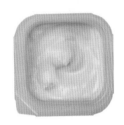

one cup of oatmeal
¼ teaspoon of sugar

one orange
2 teaspoons of sugar

one banana
3 teaspoons of sugar

Added sugar

glass of chocolate milk
3 teaspoons of sugar
+ 3 teaspoons of added sugar

small tub of fruit yogurt
3 teaspoons of sugar
+ 3 teaspoons of added sugar

**one cup of cereal,
sugar coated**
3 teaspoons of added sugar

glass of orange juice
2 teaspoons of sugar
+ 3 teaspoons of added sugar

banana muffin
3 teaspoons of sugar
+ 6 teaspoons of added sugar

How to write about your opinion

State your opinion

Think about the main question in the introduction on page 4 of this book. What is your opinion?

Research

Look for other information that you need to back up your opinion.

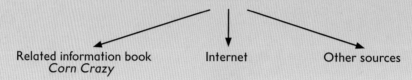

| Related information book *Corn Crazy* | Internet | Other sources |

Make a plan

Introduction

How will you "hook" the reader to get them interested?

Write a sentence that makes your opinion clear.

List reasons to support your opinion.

| Support your reason with examples. | Support your reason with examples. | Support your reason with examples. |

Conclusion

Write a sentence that makes your opinion clear. Leave your reader with a strong message.

Publish

Publish your writing.

Include some graphics or visual images.